HOW TO MAKE MONEY WITH AI

Unlocking Financial
Prosperity in the Age of
Artificial Intelligence

Evan B. Lark

Table Of Content

INTRODUCTION

      What Exactly is AI?

      How Does It Function?

      The Many Forms Of AI

      AI's Importance In Money Making

      How to Make Use of This Book

Chapter 1

Subcontract Your AI Skills

      Identifying Your AI Abilities

      Identifying freelance AI customers

      Pricing Your Freelancing Artificial Intelligence Services

      Providing High-quality Freelancing Artificial Intelligence Work

      Creating a Successful Freelance AI Career

Chapter 2

Create and Sell AI-Powered Products in

      Identifying Potential for AI-powered Products

      AI-powered Product Design And Development

      Selling And Marketing AI-powered Goods

      Case Studies

Chapter 3

Invest in AI-Powered Businesses in

      Finding AI-enabled Investing Possibilities

      Performing AI Duc Diligence

      Managing Artificial Intelligence Investments

      Case studies of successful investments in

artificial intelligence-powered firms

Chapter 4

Making Money with AI in the Future

    AI Emerging Trends

    How Artificial Intelligence is Changing the
Workplace

    Ethical implications for profiting from AI

Conclusion

INTRODUCTION

In a world where the tides of technological advancement smash on the beaches of our everyday existence, an intriguing realm that has grabbed many people's imaginations emerges artificial intelligence. This mysterious force, a modern-day miracle, has woven itself into the very fabric of our lives, transforming the landscape of our possibilities and pushing the frontiers of what we once believed was possible.

Welcome to a tour into the promising expanse of artificial intelligence, where we will set out on a mission to discover the buried treasure trove of riches and prosperity. This is more than a book; it is a road map to grasping the potential of AI and utilizing it for financial gain.

We shall unravel the mystique of AI, explain its inner workings, and explore the various paths it presents for the discriminating explorer to earn a career as you flip the pages of this book. We will chart a route through the complicated world of artificial intelligence to reveal chances for financial benefit, from freelancing your AI abilities to building and selling AI-powered wonders, from investing in the aspirations of young startups to predicting the destiny of established giants. But it does not end there. This trip is enriched with real-life success and fortitude tales. You will meet people who have changed their lives one algorithm at a time by using AI in creative and unusual ways. Their tales demonstrate AI's limitless promise as well as the transformational impact it may wield.

As you go, we will lead you through the thick forest of AI tools and resources, revealing the road to learning the skills and knowledge required to traverse this changing world. We will reveal the treasure troves of software, courses, and groups that will be your partners in your pursuit of success.

This book is more than simply a handbook; it is your mentor, a reliable guide, and a continuous companion on your journey. The route may be tortuous, and the trials may be difficult, but the benefits, my dear reader, are unfathomable.

So buckle in and be ready for a journey into a future where the artificial becomes the artisan, intelligence is harnessed for wealth, and your search for financial well-being starts. Hello and welcome to the world of "How to Make Money with AI." Your journey is waiting for you, and the possibilities are endless.

What Exactly is AI?

AI, or artificial intelligence, is a branch of computer science that tries to make computers or robots think and behave like humans.Artificial intelligence is recognized as the emulation of human cognitive functions carried out by machines, especially computer systems.Consider the possibility that a computer might comprehend and learn from information, make judgments, and even identify pictures and words.

AI enables machines to assess data, solve issues, and complete jobs without having to be explicitly programmed for each step. It has applications ranging from self-driving vehicles and voice assistants like Siri or Alexa to assisting physicians in more precisely diagnosing ailments. AI is similar to educating a computer to be intelligent and make choices on its own, which may be very beneficial in many parts of our lives.

How Does It Function?

AI systems operate through the ingestion of extensive sets of labeled training data, where they analyze the data for associations and trends, subsequently employing these patterns to make projections about future conditions.By examining millions of instances, a chatbot given text samples may learn to make realistic discussions with humans, while an image recognition program can learn to recognize and describe items in photographs. New generative AI algorithms that are quickly developing can generate realistic text, graphics, music, and other material. Here's a quick explanation of how it works:

- Data Collection: AI systems begin by collecting a large amount of information or data. Text, pictures, numbers, and sounds are all examples of data.

- Learning Patterns: The computer looks for patterns and correlations in this data. For example, it may learn that particular terms often occur together in news stories.

- Model Development: AI develops models or rules based on what it has learned. These models assist computers in making predictions or choices. It may, for example, anticipate the subject of an article based on the words used.

- Testing and Improving: Artificial intelligence systems are tested on fresh data to determine whether they produce correct predictions or conclusions. In case of an error, they take it as an opportunity to enhance and grow.

- Continuous Learning: AI is similar to a student who continues to study and improve over time. The more data it collects and learns, the smarter it grows.

The Many Forms Of AI

Based on its capabilities and functions, artificial intelligence may be divided into three categories. Let's break down these kinds in an easy-to-understand manner:

- Artificial Narrow Intelligence (ANI) (Artificial Narrow Intelligence): - Consider this AI with a specified task. It excels at one particular task.

- A kind of Narrow AI is, for example, your smartphone's voice assistant, such as Siri or Alexa. It's great at answering questions and setting alarms, but it can't drive or cook.

- General AI (Artificial General Intelligence - AGI): AKA "all-around" AI. It is capable of doing a broad variety of duties, much like a person.

- Consider an AI that can converse with you, solve arithmetic problems, compose tales, and even teach itself new things. We don't yet have AGI, but it's a long-term aim.

- Superintelligent AI (Artificial Superintelligence - ASI): This is the AI equivalent of a superhero. It is much more intelligent than any person and can swiftly solve complicated issues.

- If ASI ever arises, it can outperform human intellect and achieve things we cannot even comprehend now.

You have Narrow AI, which is excellent at specialized jobs, General AI, which is a jack-of-all-trades, and the concept of Superintelligent AI, which is very intelligent. In our everyday lives, we largely encounter Narrow AI, whereas General and Superintelligent AI are still on the horizon.

AI's Importance In Money Making

AI is becoming more crucial for profit because it provides strong tools to organizations and people, assisting them in a variety of ways:

- Efficiency: AI can accomplish things more quickly and precisely than humans. This implies that organizations may do more in less time, lowering costs and improving revenues.

- Data Analysis: AI can sift through massive volumes of data to uncover insights and patterns that people would overlook. This enables firms to make educated choices and efficiently target their goods or services.

- Personalization: AI can personalize goods and services to the tastes of individual customers. This results in happy consumers and increased revenue.

- Automation: Artificial intelligence (AI) may automate tedious jobs, allowing individuals to concentrate on more creative and important work. This may lower labor expenses while increasing output.

- Innovation: AI may promote innovation by allowing the invention of previously unimaginable new goods, services, and business models.

- Competitive Advantage: Early adopters of AI may acquire a competitive advantage. They can provide better services, be more nimble, and swiftly adjust to changing market circumstances.

In essence, artificial intelligence (AI) is a smart assistant that assists organizations and people in working smarter, making more money, and staying ahead in a fast-paced, data-driven environment. This is why it is becoming more important in the field of earning money.

How to Make Use of This Book

Here's a short and straightforward way to using this book effectively:
- Begin with the Fundamentals: Begin by reading the "Introduction" section. This gives

you an outline of the book's topic and why AI is vital for producing money. It sets the tone for your adventure.

- Learn about AI by diving into "How to Make Money with AI." Read the chapters in this area to learn about the numerous ways you may utilize AI to make money. It's similar to taking multiple roads on your financial journey.

- Study Real-Life Examples: In "Case Studies," learn about the real-life experiences of individuals who have effectively employed AI for financial advantage. These tales provide both inspiration and practical advice.

- Arm Yourself: In "AI Tools and Resources," learn about the tools, courses, and groups that may assist you in developing AI abilities. It's similar to packing your belongings for a trip.

- Look to the Future: The "Conclusion" chapter provides an outlook on how to make money using AI in the future. It's like a compass pointing you in the direction of new prospects.

- Take Action: Take notes, scribble down thoughts, and evaluate how the material relates to your objectives as you read. This book is your route map; modify it to suit your needs.

- Continuous Learning: Keep in mind that AI is always growing. Even after you've finished the book, keep your curiosity and learning going. The world of AI is dynamic, and keeping current is critical to success.

This book will be your trusted guide on your journey to harness AI for financial advantage. As you begin on your road to producing money using AI, use it as a reference, source of inspiration, and guidance.

Chapter 1

Subcontract Your AI Skills

Freelancing your AI abilities is employing your artificial intelligence ability to work on projects for several customers, much like a freelance artist or writer. You may provide your AI expertise and skills to companies or people who want assistance with AI-related activities. It's a versatile approach to earn money while sharing your AI skills with others.

Identifying Your AI Abilities

Identifying your AI talents is an important step toward successfully using artificial intelligence. It all comes down to identifying and comprehending your AI capabilities and skills. This process is similar to discovering your particular capabilities, similar to how a musician discovers their musical ability or an athlete recognizes their strengths in a given sport. Here's how you can go about it more specifically:

- Self-Evaluation: Begin by carefully considering what you know and what you can perform in the field of artificial intelligence. Are you skilled in artificial intelligence methods such as machine learning, computer vision, or natural language processing? Determine the specific areas in which you have extensive expertise.

- Previous Experiences: Consider your previous AI-related experiences and initiatives. Have you completed AI projects, created AI models, or used AI approaches to tackle real-world problems? Your track record may demonstrate your practical abilities.

- Curiosity and Passion: Consider what areas of AI really tickle your attention. Your interest in a certain area often leads to your inherent skills. If you have a natural interest in AI ethics, robotics, or deep learning, this is an indication of your possible skill set.

- input and Mentoring: Seek input from AI mentors, coworkers, or peers. They may provide insights into your strengths and areas of strength. They may highlight your exceptional problem-solving talents, coding expertise, or ability to convey complicated AI ideas to others.

- Continuous Learning: Recognize that the area of artificial intelligence is always changing. Recognizing areas where you want to learn and extend your knowledge is also part of identifying your AI talents. This may include taking classes, attending seminars, or acquiring hands-on experience.

The importance of defining your AI talents may be found in the actual implementations of this knowledge. It acts as a map of your talents in the enormous world of artificial intelligence, pointing you toward the correct career paths, initiatives, or additional studies that correspond with your strengths. Whether you're thinking of freelancing your AI talents, producing AI-driven products, investing in AI enterprises, or pursuing a career in AI research, knowing your AI strengths allows you to make educated choices and maximize your distinct abilities. It's like having a customized compass to keep you on track in the ever-changing world of artificial intelligence.

Identifying freelance AI customers

Finding freelancing AI customers is an important part of utilizing your AI talents to make money on your own. It's like embarking on a mission to find chances where you can use your AI skills to benefit people while also earning money.

Here's a more in-depth approach to finding freelancing AI clients:

1. Start your experience on online freelancing marketplaces such as Upwork, Fiverr, or Freelancer. These platforms function similarly to busy marketplaces where customers from all around the globe publish AI-related tasks. You may establish a profile displaying your AI expertise, explore open projects, and pitch prospective customers.

2. Job Boards for Specific Industries and AI specializations: Some industries and AI specializations have their own job boards and forums. For example, if you specialize in artificial intelligence for healthcare, you may locate chances on healthcare-specific job sites or forums where experts discuss their requirements.

3. Networking is a very useful technology. Attend AI conferences and seminars, or join online AI forums.

You may network with possible clients or others who may be able to recommend you for assignments.

4. Cold Outreach: There are instances when you may go out to firms or people who might benefit from your AI talents. Make a convincing proposal that explains how your AI knowledge can help them address particular challenges or enhance their operations.

5. Personal Website and Portfolio: Creating a personal website exhibiting your AI work, as well as a portfolio of former projects, may reassure prospective customers. They may view your qualifications as well as samples of your work.

6. LinkedIn: LinkedIn is a great professional networking tool. Optimize your LinkedIn profile to emphasize your AI talents, and connect with prospective customers or people who may introduce you to freelancing prospects.

7. Some organizations and consultancies specialize in connecting freelancing AI workers with customers. Consider collaborating with such organizations to get access to a pool of customers looking for AI expertise.

8. Word of Mouth: Never underestimate the power of referrals. If you have already achieved excellent outcomes on past projects, your delighted customers may refer you to others. Develop these connections.

9. Continuous Learning and Improvement: Stay current on AI developments and technology. The more you study and improve, the more enticing you will be to prospective customers.

10. Maintain a high degree of professionalism in all contacts with customers. This involves effective communication, fulfilling deadlines, and producing high-quality results.

It's like going on a treasure hunt to find freelancing AI clients. It's a chance to contribute your AI expertise, solve real-world issues, and make a livelihood doing something you're passionate about. Exploring different pathways and always honing your talents can open doors to a world of freelance AI jobs, allowing you to prosper in this dynamic area.

Pricing Your Freelancing Artificial Intelligence Services

Pricing your freelancing AI services is an important step toward success as an AI freelancer. It's akin to determining the appropriate monetary value for your treasure mine of AI talents and knowledge. Here's an in-depth guide on efficiently pricing your services:

- Understand Your Expenses: Start with understanding your own expenses. This covers your living expenditures, taxes, any software or equipment you utilize, as well as any additional outlays. recognizing your charges is similar to recognizing the price you need to continue your freelancing firm.

- Market research: Find out how much other AI freelancers charge for comparable services. This is similar to learning from people who have traveled on the same journey. It might give you an idea of how competitive the prices are in the AI freelancing sector.

- Value-Based Pricing: Think about the value you bring to your customers. Your services are very valued if your AI talents can save a company thousands of dollars or help it create income. Clients are often prepared to pay a premium for high-value services.

- Hourly vs. Project-Based: Determine whether you want to charge customers by the hour or by the project. Hourly rates provide a consistent stream of revenue, but project-based pricing provides more certainty for both you and the customer.

- Negotiating: Be open to negotiating while maintaining a consistent price structure. This indicates that you are adaptable yet not hesitant about your pricing. Clients may have specified budgets, in which case a well-structured negotiation may be mutually advantageous.

- Pricing levels: Provide a variety of pricing levels depending on the scope of work or supplementary services. This is analogous to offering alternatives to customers with diverse wants. A basic package may be less expensive, but premium packages may contain more features.

- Trial Periods: For new customers, consider giving a trial term at a reduced fee. This is similar to giving them a taste of your knowledge. If people realize the value of your services throughout the trial period, they are more inclined to continue using them.

- Review and adjust your price regularly. You may alter your fees to reflect your improved worth as your talents and reputation rise. It's like climbing the success ladder and earning more as you go.

- Transparency: Be open and honest about your price. This fosters client trust. Unexpected fees or penalties might tarnish your reputation.

- Contract conditions: In your contracts, clearly specify the conditions, including payment schedules and any extra expenses. This guarantees that you and your customers both have a shared grasp of the financial issues.

Keep in mind that pricing your freelancing AI services is a fluid process. It necessitates continual examination and change as your knowledge and experience expand. The idea is to strike a balance in which you are adequately rewarded for your knowledge while your customers believe they are getting good value for their money. Your price plan acts as a compass, guiding you to a successful freelance AI career by achieving that balance.

Providing High-quality Freelancing Artificial Intelligence Work

Delivering high-quality freelance AI work is the foundation of a successful career as an AI freelancer. It's like making a masterpiece that not only pleases your clientele but also boosts your industry reputation. Here's a detailed tutorial on how to constantly give excellent AI services:

- Understand Your Client's Needs: Start by completely knowing your client's needs. This is similar to determining the client's vision and expectations. Schedule meetings, ask questions, and ensure you have a thorough knowledge of the project's goals.

- Data Quality: Data is the lifeblood of AI. Make certain that the data you utilize to train your AI models is of good quality and relevant to the job at hand. This is like an artist having the finest paint and canvas. For reliable findings, clean, well-organized data is required.

- Model Selection: Select the best AI model for the job. It's analogous to an artist picking the proper brush or instrument. Different AI models are more effective for different challenges. To guarantee efficacy, make an educated decision.

- Testing and Validation: Put your AI models through rigorous testing. This is analogous to continuously evaluating and improving your artwork. Ascertain that your models are correct and operate as planned. To assess their performance, use validation datasets and metrics.

- Documentation: Thoroughly document your efforts. Keep track of the actions you've done, the parameters you've used, and any problems you've run into. This documentation functions similarly to an artist's notebook, assisting you in replicating and troubleshooting your work.

- Communication: Keep clear and open lines of communication open with your customer. Provide frequent progress reports on the project. It's similar to keeping your art collector updated on the progress of the painting. Transparency builds trust.

- Quality Control: Put in place quality control procedures. Examine your AI work for flaws, prejudice, and ethical issues in the same way that an artist scrutinizes every aspect of their work.

- Deliver on time: Follow project timetables and deadlines. Reliable delivery is analogous to an artist producing the artwork on time. It fosters trust and dependability.

- Incorporate input: Be receptive to input and eager to make required changes. This is analogous to an artist improving their work in response to criticism. Client input may help you develop your AI products.

- Ethical Considerations: Make sure your AI development follows ethical rules and protects user privacy. Ethical practices are analogous to an artist's dedication to societal duty via their work.

- AI is a dynamic discipline that requires continuous learning. Keep up with the newest innovations, tools, and approaches. Your continual learning, like that of an artist experimenting with different media, keeps your work fresh and current.

- Post-Project Assistance: Assist after the project has been completed. It's analogous to an artist giving help if the artwork needs repair. Make yourself ready to answer any concerns or inquiries that may occur.

As an AI freelancer, your signature is delivering high-quality freelance AI work. It's not only about completing the job; it's about providing long-term value to your customers and building a reputation that attracts new prospects. Your dedication to quality is your paintbrush, painting a picture of perfection in the realm of AI freelancing.

Creating a Successful Freelance AI Career

Building a successful freelance AI job is similar to building a well-designed and robust structure. It requires a deliberate blend of abilities, preparation, and constant work. Here's a comprehensive guide to launching a successful career as a freelance AI professional:

- Skills Development: Your skill set is the cornerstone of your AI career. Learn and enhance your AI abilities in areas such as machine learning, data analysis, and deep learning continuously. It's like creating a solid foundation for your career.

- Consider concentrating on an area of AI such as natural language processing, computer vision, or healthcare AI. Specialization is similar to choosing an architectural style for your building; it distinguishes you and attracts particular clientele.

- Understand the AI freelancing industry via market research. Investigate the demand for AI services, the competition, and the prices charged by others. This is analogous to surveying the terrain to choose the best site for your structure.

- Portfolio Creation: Create a portfolio of your greatest work and projects. This portfolio, like your building's magnificent façade, provides customers with a view of your skills.

- Building a solid professional network in the AI community. Attend conferences, participate in online forums, and network with colleagues and possible clients. Networking entails making links with nearby firms.

- Online Presence: Establish a strong online presence. A professional website, a LinkedIn page, and a presence on AI-related platforms are all required. It's like having a well-lit signboard for your building that makes it easy to find.

- Pricing Strategy: Consider your charges carefully. Whether you choose hourly or project-based pricing, be sure it represents your talents and the value you provide. Setting a reasonable rent for your building's areas is analogous to your pricing approach.

- Marketing: Effectively promote your services. To reach out to prospective customers, use content marketing, social media, and internet advertising. Marketing is the process of raising awareness about the services provided by your building.

- Client connections: Develop solid client connections. The cornerstones of trust are clear communication, dependability, and high-quality work. Building strong customer connections is similar to establishing long-term ties with your renters.

- Financial Management: Take good care of your money. Keep track of your costs, taxes, and earnings. Maintaining your building's financial health requires good financial management.

- Maintain professionalism in all of your dealings, whether online or offline. Maintaining professionalism is similar to keeping your facility clean, well-maintained, and attractive.

- AI is a constantly expanding discipline that requires continuous learning. Keep up to speed on the newest developments and trends. Continuous learning is analogous to upgrading and updating your structure to suit current requirements.
- Incorporating Client input: Be receptive to client input and change appropriately. Feedback is similar to doing inspections to find and correct problems in your building.

- Considerations for Ethics: Maintain ethical standards in your AI work. Make certain that your initiatives are ethical and take into account social ramifications. Ethical issues are comparable to construction rules and safety precautions for your project.

- Consider diversifying your revenue streams, such as providing AI training or consulting services. Diversification is like adding different wings to your structure for different functions.

- Long-Term Goals: Have a long-term goal in mind for your freelancing AI job. Make a plan for the future and establish attainable targets. Your vision serves as the blueprint for your building's progress and growth.

Building a successful freelance AI profession takes consistent work, flexibility, and dedication to quality. Your AI career grows with each project, customer, and accomplishment, much as the quality and reputation of a building do. It's a framework constructed with passion, talent, and dedication, and when done well, it can stand tall in the competitive world of AI freelancing.

Chapter 2

Create and Sell
AI-Powered Products in

Creating and marketing AI-powered goods entails creating smart software, chatbots, or useful devices that employ artificial intelligence to improve people's lives. You create these items and then sell them like any other thing to benefit others while also making money. It is about fusing technology with practical answers.

Identifying Potential for AI-powered Products

Identifying AI-powered product prospects is like seeking hidden jewels in the technological world. It entails identifying areas where artificial intelligence may be used to generate unique and valued goods. Here's a comprehensive approach to spotting these opportunities:

- Market Research: Begin by learning about the market. Determine which sectors or areas might benefit from AI to solve issues, improve processes, or enhance experiences. It's similar to studying a map before embarking on a treasure hunt.

- Consumer Wants and Needs: Pay attention to what consumers want and need. Look for areas of pain or difficulty that AI might help with. These requirements are similar to the hints that lead you to the prize.

- Analyze what your competitors are doing in the AI sector. Identify holes in the market where your unique offering may provide something unusual or better. It's like discovering an unexplored area on a treasure map.

- AI Technology Trends: Keep up with the latest AI technology trends. New developments may pave the way for novel goods. Being aware of these tendencies is analogous to understanding the instruments you will need for your treasure quest.

- Brainstorm Ideas: Form a group or work alone to develop AI product ideas. Consider how artificial intelligence (AI) may make people's life simpler, more efficient, or more pleasurable. These brainstorming sessions are analogous to planning your route to the prize.

- Create a prototype or minimal viable product (MVP) when you've had an idea. To obtain feedback, test it with prospective consumers. This is similar to digging for treasure to determine whether you're on the correct route.

- User-Centered Design: Emphasize the user experience. Make sure your AI-powered solution is easy to use and addresses real-world challenges. It's similar to making a treasure box that is simple to open and holds precious stuff.

- Iterate and refine: Make use of customer input to enhance your product. Iteration is similar to polishing and refining the treasure you've discovered to make it even more precious.
- Monetization Strategy: Figure out how you'll monetize your AI-powered product. Is it going to be a one-time payment, a subscription, or something else? This is

analogous to determining the worth of the treasure you've unearthed.

- Legal and ethical considerations: Make certain that your product conforms with all applicable laws and ethical standards. It's similar to ensuring that your wealth is gained and shared appropriately.

- Launch and marketing: Show the world your AI-powered product. Make a marketing plan to reach your intended audience. It's similar like revealing your riches to the public.

- Continuous Improvement: Continue to improve your product in response to consumer input and technology improvements. This is like always adding additional diamonds to your treasure box.

- Identifying potential for AI-powered products is a fascinating pursuit that demands a sharp eye for unmet needs and a creative mind to generate solutions. When you identify these possibilities and produce excellent AI-powered solutions, it's like discovering gems that not only help people but also reward your inventive efforts financially.

AI-powered Product Design And Development

Designing and developing AI-powered goods is similar to creating a one-of-a-kind and sophisticated tool that uses artificial intelligence to tackle particular issues or improve user experiences. Here's a detailed instruction on how to make such items:

- Begin with a clear idea of the issue you want to address or the benefit you want to make. This is similar to agreeing on the purpose and usefulness of your product, which is similar to an architect's plan.

- Market research includes researching your target audience as well as your rivals. Recognize their wants and needs. This study is analogous to knowing the context in which your product will be utilized as architects do when designing a structure.

- Data Collection: AI is dependent on data, thus acquiring relevant and high-quality data. It's like acquiring the best ingredients for the development of your goods.

- Choose the right AI approaches for your product, such as machine learning, natural language processing, or computer vision. This is analogous to picking the appropriate tools and equipment for the construction of your product.

- Prototyping: Make a model of your product. This is a condensed version that will allow you to test your ideas and functionality. It's similar to developing a model of a structure before starting the real construction.

- Develop the key AI algorithms and incorporate them into your product. This procedure is analogous to building the framework and structure of your product.

- Design of User Interface (UI) and User Experience (UX): Create an intuitive and user-friendly interface. This is analogous to planning the layout and look of a structure to guarantee its residents' accessibility and comfort.

- Testing and Quality Assurance: Test your AI-powered product thoroughly for functionality, accuracy, and any faults. It's analogous to assessing a building to verify it satisfies safety requirements.

- User input: Collect input from users during testing and make any required changes. This is analogous to soliciting feedback from prospective residents to improve their living experience.

- Scalability: As your product expands, ensure that it can manage greater use and data. This is analogous to constructing a structure that can house additional residents in the future.

- Implement strong data security procedures to secure user information and ensure privacy. Installing security systems in a structure to safeguard its people is analogous.

- Legal and ethical considerations: Comply with data use and AI rules and ethical norms. This is analogous to following building regulations and ethical standards in construction.

- Monetization Strategy: Determine your price scheme, whether it's a one-time buy, a subscription, or something else. It's similar to calculating a building's rent or selling price.

- Launch and marketing: Make your AI-powered product available to the public. Make a marketing plan to reach your intended audience. This is analogous to introducing a new building to prospective occupants.

- Maintenance and updates: Maintain and update your product regularly to repair bugs and add new features. This is analogous to maintaining and remodeling a structure to keep it in good shape.

AI-powered product design and development is a creative and technical process that requires a thorough grasp of consumer demands, AI capabilities, and technology breakthroughs. You, like an architect, develop and create AI-powered products to deliver solutions and improve people's lives while providing you with the chance to prosper in the field of AI innovation.

Selling And Marketing AI-powered Goods

Marketing and selling AI-powered goods is akin to exposing the world to a wonderful innovation and persuading people of its advantages. It entails using a calculated strategy to make your product recognized and appealing to your target audience. Here's a comprehensive approach to efficiently marketing and selling AI-powered products:

- 1Identifying Your Ideal Customers: Learn about your ideal customers' wants and preferences. It's like knowing who is most likely to be interested in your innovation.

- Unique Selling Proposition (USP): Identify what distinguishes your AI-powered solution from the competitors. Showcase how it addresses particular issues or enhances the user experience. Your USP is the distinguishing trait that distinguishes your innovation.

- Pricing Strategy: Choose a pricing plan that corresponds to the value your product provides. Make that the price system is competitive and fair, whether it's a one-time purchase, subscription, or other. Your pricing approach is similar to determining the value of your idea.

- Marketing Materials: Create marketing materials that describe the characteristics, advantages, and operation of your product. Use simple, appealing language. These resources serve as your invention's user handbook.

- Create an online presence for your goods by creating a professional website or landing page. Optimize it for search engines (SEO) to guarantee that it can be found online. Your website serves as a showcase for visitors to learn about and experiment with your idea.

- Material marketing entails sharing helpful and valuable material about your product. Blog entries, videos, and infographics may assist in educating and developing trust with prospective clients. Creating instructional materials for your innovation is analogous to content marketing.

- Social Media Marketing: Connect with your audience via social media networks. Share product updates, interact with people, and build a community around your product. Hosting events to exhibit your idea is similar to social media marketing.

- Email Marketing: Create your email list and give subscribers frequent updates, advice, and special offers. Email marketing is similar to sending out newsletters to those who are interested in your idea.

- Paid Advertising: To reach a larger audience, invest in internet advertising such as pay-per-click (PPC) campaigns. It's similar to putting ads in high-traffic locations to attract prospective buyers.

- Create dedicated landing pages and sales funnels that take visitors through the experience of learning about your product, appreciating its value, and making a purchase decision. This is equivalent to offering a clear way for people to investigate and purchase your innovation.

- Product demonstrations and Trials: Provide free product demonstrations or trials. This enables prospective buyers to have a personal look at it. Demonstrations and trials are similar to test drives for your innovation.

- Customer Service: Provide great customer service in response to requests, problems, and difficulties. A responsive support crew is equivalent to your innovation having a customer service hotline.

- User Testimonials and Reviews: Encourage pleased consumers to post reviews and testimonials. Positive feedback is equivalent to word-of-mouth endorsements for your idea.

- Affiliate marketing entails working with affiliates to promote your product in return for a commission. It's similar to having a team of sales representatives who participate in the earnings from each transaction.

- Analytics and Optimization: Track the effectiveness of your marketing activities using data and analytics. Optimize your tactics depending on what is most effective. It's similar to fine-tuning your sales and marketing strategies to optimize the success of your idea.

- Scalability: As your product acquires momentum, plan for scalability. Ascertain that your marketing and sales systems are capable of handling rising demand. It's similar to planning to fulfill the needs of an expanding consumer base.

Marketing and selling AI-powered goods need a well-thought-out and multifaceted strategy. You're exposing your creative product to the world, proving its worth, and encouraging buyers to experience the advantages of your AI-powered innovation in the same way that a successful creator advertises and sells their idea. It is a process that combines creativity, communication, and strategic thinking to ensure your product's commercial success.

Case Studies

Case studies of successful AI-powered goods are similar to tales of technologies that altered industries and improved people's lives by using artificial intelligence. These real-world examples show how AI may be used to provide unique and meaningful solutions. Here are some in-depth case studies:

- Alexa, Amazon:
  - Issue: Smart home control and voice recognition.
  - Solution: Amazon's Alexa, which is powered by natural language processing, allows users to use voice commands to operate smart devices, play music, set alarms, and answer questions.
  - Result: Alexa has become a household name, changing how people interact with technology and their homes.

- Autopilot by Tesla:
  - Issue: Improving vehicle safety and convenience.
  - Solution: Tesla's Autopilot technology enables sophisticated driver-assistance features and partial self-driving capabilities by using machine learning and computer vision.
  - Result: Tesla's Autopilot has raised the bar for vehicle automation and is a critical component in the adoption of self-driving technology.

- Netflix's Recommendation Engine:
  - Issue: Customizing content suggestions.

- Solution: Netflix analyzes user preferences and watching behavior using AI algorithms to provide personalized movie and TV program suggestions.

- Outcome: By keeping viewers interested and pleased, our AI-driven recommendation engine greatly adds to Netflix's success.

- IBM Watson for Cancer Care:
  - Issue: Individualized cancer therapy suggestions.

  - Solution: IBM Watson for Oncology uses artificial intelligence to examine massive quantities of medical literature, patient information, and clinical trial data to provide therapy recommendations to oncologists.

  - Outcome: Watson for Oncology has increased cancer care accuracy and efficiency, benefitting both patients and healthcare professionals.

- Language Translation by Google:
  - Issue: Breaking down linguistic barriers.

  - Solution: To produce reliable translations between more than 100 languages, Google Translate combines deep learning and neural machine translation.

- Outcome: Google's translation service has simplified and expanded worldwide cross-language communication.

- Robot Vacuum Roomba:
  - Issue: Efficient and self-sufficient house cleaning.
  - Solution: Equipped with AI-powered sensors, the Roomba navigates houses, recognizes obstructions, and cleans floors automatically.
  - Result: Roomba has become a home need, automating a tedious activity and simplifying everyday living.

- Music Recommendations from Spotify:
  - Issue: Customizing music playlists.
  - Solution: Spotify analyzes users' listening patterns and recommends tailored playlists and song suggestions based on machine learning.
  - Result: The platform's AI-powered music suggestions keep users interested and returning for more.

These case studies show how AI-powered technologies have transformed sectors ranging from smart home devices to healthcare and entertainment. They demonstrate the power of artificial intelligence to solve complicated issues, improve user experiences, and build technologies that will become indispensable in our everyday lives. Investigating these triumphs reveals important insights about the strength of AI and its role in determining the future of technology and innovation.

Chapter 3

Invest in AI-Powered Businesses in

Investing in AI-powered firms entails pouring money into companies that employ artificial intelligence to develop new goods and services. It's similar to investing in firms on the bleeding edge of technology, with the potential for tremendous growth and financial gains as AI advances and transforms many sectors.

Finding AI-enabled Investing Possibilities

Recognizing interesting avenues in the ever-expanding AI ecosystem is similar to identifying AI-powered financial prospects. It entails identifying companies and projects that use artificial intelligence to promote development and innovation. Here's a comprehensive guide to identifying these investing opportunities:

- Begin by doing market research on the AI market. Recognize the areas and sectors where artificial intelligence is having a substantial influence, such as healthcare, banking, or e-commerce. It's similar to analyzing a map to find a rich area for investment.

- Keep up to speed with AI developments and upcoming technology. Investigate how AI is being used in many industries, from machine learning in finance to computer vision in healthcare. These tendencies serve as indicators of possible investment regions.

- Startup environment: Learn about the startup environment. AI startups often provide novel solutions. Look for firms that have distinct offers and strong growth prospects. This is comparable to scouting for young and promising talent.

- Financial Performance: Examine the financial performance of firms driven by AI. Examine their revenue growth, profit margins, and market share. It's similar to researching a company's track record before investing.

- Competitive edge: Determine whether or not the AI-powered company has a competitive edge. This might include proprietary algorithms, data, or specialist knowledge. It's similar to assessing a prospective investment's capabilities and resources.

- Leadership Team: Assess the leadership team's AI competence and capacity to carry out the business's strategy. Strong leadership is equivalent to having experienced commanders on board your investment vessel.

- Partnerships and Collaborations: Look into the partnerships and collaborations that the company has developed. Partnerships with well-known firms may signal credibility and prospective development. These relationships function similarly to alliances throughout your investing path.

- Check to see whether the company has any valuable AI-related patents or intellectual property. This may be a very useful item. It's similar to determining ownership of land and resources in an investment.

- Ethical Considerations: Make certain that the AI-powered company follows ethical rules and legislation. Responsible practices function similarly to legal frameworks for your investment.

- Diversification: Consider spreading your AI investments across many industries or enterprises. Diversification is similar to spreading your assets over other crops to reduce risk.

- 11. Risk Assessment: Recognize the risks involved with AI investments, such as market swings, technology advancements, and regulatory obstacles. Identifying risks is like planning for inclement weather on your financial trip.

- Long-Term Vision: Evaluate the company's long-term vision and scalability. Consider how artificial intelligence breakthroughs may affect the company's growth. This is analogous to assessing the long-term viability of your investment.

Identifying artificial intelligence-powered investment prospects requires a combination of research, industry expertise, and strategic thinking. You search for promising AI enterprises with the potential to produce substantial returns on investment and contribute to the continued advancement of artificial intelligence, much as an explorer seeks out undiscovered places for exploration.

Performing AI Due Diligence

AI due diligence is the process of extensively assessing the attributes and prospects of an AI-powered investment opportunity before committing to your resources. It entails a planned procedure that ensures you make educated investing selections. Here's a comprehensive approach to doing AI due diligence:

- Business grasp: Gain a thorough grasp of the AI-powered company, its basic activities, and its distinguishing features. It's similar to researching the history and nature of the land you're thinking about investing in.

- Technology Assessment: Evaluate the technology that underpins the company. Determine if the AI algorithms, tools, and models deployed give a competitive edge. This is comparable to inspecting the soil quality and accessible resources on the property.

- Data Assets: Look into the data assets on which the company depends. High-quality data is required for AI to succeed. Examine how the firm gathers, maintains, and uses data. It's similar to assessing the land's water supply and irrigation capability.

- Market Analysis: Examine the industry in which the company works. Determine the size, potential for expansion, and competitive environment. Understanding the demand and market circumstances for your possible investment is analogous to this.

- Examine the intellectual property of the company, such as patents, trademarks, and proprietary algorithms. Ensure that its important AI assets are safeguarded. This is equivalent to confirming legal title and rights to the land.

- Regulatory Compliance: Determine whether or not the company conforms with AI-related rules, privacy laws, and ethical norms. Check for any legal impediments. This is equivalent to certifying that the investment complies with current rules and regulations.

- Financial Analysis: Examine the company's financial performance, including sales, costs, and profitability. It's similar to doing a financial audit on the investment.

- client Base: Learn about your client base and user happiness. Customer satisfaction indicates a solid corporate basis. This is equivalent to understanding your neighborhood and possible renters for your investment.

- Team competence: Evaluate the leadership and technical team's competence. Strong AI expertise and experience are essential. It's similar to ensuring that your land's farmers and work crew are trained and experienced.

- Partnerships and Collaborations: Look into the partnerships and collaborations of the company. These might be indicators of credibility and prospective development. It's similar to looking for prospective company partnerships in your investing region.

- Reports on Due Diligence: Examine due diligence reports from external specialists or auditing firms. They may give useful information on the company's strengths and problems. These studies are similar to talking with experts regarding the possibilities of the property.

- Scalability: Consider the business's scalability. Assess its ability to develop and adapt to changing market circumstances. It's similar to determining the land's potential for growth and development.

- Risk Assessment: Identify and analyze possible investment risks such as market instability, technical developments, and competition. It's similar to planning for unforeseen difficulties in your investment.

AI due diligence is a thorough procedure that ensures your investment is aligned with your goals and is built on a strong foundation of knowledge and expertise. To guarantee a successful and beneficial investment, just as a farmer assesses every part of the soil before planting seeds, you evaluate every component of an AI-powered firm before investing your resources.

Managing Artificial Intelligence Investments

Managing AI investments is like tending to a garden of possibilities. It entails monitoring your investments in AI-powered firms and projects to ensure their growth and success. Here's a comprehensive approach to efficiently managing your AI investments:

- Portfolio Diversification: Just as a gardener produces a variety of plants to reduce risk, spread your AI investments across several industries and enterprises. This reduces the effect of any one area's possible downfall.

- Monitoring Performance: Monitor the performance of your AI investments regularly. Maintain an eye on critical KPIs, financial reports, and market developments. This is analogous to keeping track of the health and development of plants in your garden.

- Rebalancing: Rebalance your AI investing portfolio regularly. Adjust your holdings to maintain a portfolio that is consistent with your investing objectives and risk tolerance. It's similar to trimming and rearranging your garden plants to preserve equilibrium.

- Keeping Up to Date: Stay current on AI developments and technical breakthroughs. Knowledge is a gardening tool that may assist you in making educated choices and adapting to changing situations.

- Risk Management: Assess and manage the risks associated with your AI investments on an ongoing basis. This includes securing your assets against possible hazards, similar to protecting plants from pests and illnesses.

- Consider consulting with financial specialists or investment advisers who specialize in AI-related investments. Their knowledge is equivalent to speaking with an experienced gardener who can advise you on how to care for your garden.

- Long-Term Perspective: Keep your AI investments in a long-term perspective. Make no rash judgments based on short-term market volatility. AI investments may need time to mature and provide profits, much like a garden does.

- Tax Planning: Develop tax-advantaged methods for your AI investments. Reduce your tax responsibilities to optimize your earnings, just like you would with your garden.

- Reinvesting: Reinvest earnings or dividends from your AI assets to take advantage of compounding returns. It's similar to utilizing garden seeds to develop more plants and extend your garden.

- Continuous Learning: Maintain your curiosity and continue to learn about AI breakthroughs. This is analogous to experimenting with new gardening methods and finding better ways to care for your plants.

- Ethical Considerations: Make sure your AI investments are consistent with your ethical principles. Invest in companies that adhere to ethical and responsible procedures, much like a gardener does for the environment.

- Exit Strategies: Create exit plans for your AI investments. Determine the circumstances under which you would sell or divest from a certain investment. It's similar to determining when to harvest your garden's fruits.

- Resilience: Be able to withstand market swings. Maintain adaptability and calm while managing AI investments, much like a gardener does in response to changing weather conditions.

- Maintain a balanced attitude when it comes to AI investments and other financial assets. Diversify your financial garden for a well-balanced portfolio.

Managing AI investments is a dynamic and continuing activity, similar to caring for a seasonal garden. You can nurture your AI investments to bloom and produce the benefits of financial success while contributing to the progress of AI and technology with a smart and educated approach.

Case studies of successful investments in artificial intelligence-powered firms

Case studies of successful investments in AI-powered firms are similar to tales of astute investors who discovered attractive prospects in the field of artificial intelligence and profited from their foresight. These real-world examples demonstrate how wise investing selections may result in significant financial advantages. Here are some in-depth case studies:

- Google's investment in DeepMind:
  - Background: In 2014, Google purchased DeepMind, a London-based AI firm.
  - Investment Strategy: Google recognized the value of DeepMind's sophisticated AI algorithms and machine learning skills. Google was able to expand its AI skills as a result of the purchase, notably in healthcare and gaming.

- - Outcome: DeepMind's AI technology has been essential in the development of AI systems for healthcare, such as illness diagnosis and patient deterioration prediction. The investment has elevated Google to the forefront of AI-powered healthcare solutions.

- Alibaba's SenseTime Investment:
  - Background: In 2018, Alibaba invested in SenseTime, a Chinese AI firm.
  - Investment Strategy: Alibaba noticed SenseTime's AI technology's promise in face recognition, driverless cars, and other areas. The investment sought to strengthen Alibaba's cloud and e-commerce operations, as well as to incorporate AI into a variety of services.
  - End result: SenseTime has grown to become one of the world's premier AI firms, with applications in surveillance, finance, and healthcare. With its investment, Alibaba is now able to provide AI-powered solutions across its platforms.

- SoftBank's Boston Dynamics Investment:

- Background: In 2017, SoftBank purchased Boston Dynamics, a robotics and artificial intelligence business.
- Investment Strategy: SoftBank identified Boston Dynamics' superior robotics and artificial intelligence (AI) technology's promise in a variety of sectors, including logistics, construction, and healthcare.
- Outcome: Boston Dynamics has continued to advance in robotics, and its products are used in logistics automation, inspection, and research. SoftBank has positioned itself as a significant participant in AI-driven robotics as a result of the investment.

- Warren Buffett's Apple Investment:
    - Background: Warren Buffett's Berkshire Hathaway made significant investments in Apple.
    - Investment Strategy: While not an AI investment, Buffett noted Apple's significant efforts in AI and machine learning for its goods and services. This investment was made because of Apple's overall strength and its rising dependence on artificial intelligence.
    - Outcome: Apple's artificial intelligence-driven technologies, such as Siri

and machine learning algorithms, have improved user experiences and contributed to the company's constant growth.

- Tencent's Investment in Meituan-Dianping: What Does It Mean?
Tencent has invested in Meituan-Dianping, a Chinese group-buying and meal-delivery website.
- Investment Strategy: Tencent regarded Meituan-Dianping's data analytics and AI technologies as having the ability to improve user suggestions and delivery efficiency.
- Result: Meituan-Dianping's AI-powered suggestions and delivery logistics have increased its market share and profitability, transforming it into a formidable force in the food delivery and online services industries.

These case studies demonstrate how strategically investing in AI-powered enterprises has resulted in major improvements and financial benefits. They emphasize the necessity of recognizing prospective possibilities, comprehending the potential effect of artificial intelligence technologies, and matching investments with wider corporate strategy. Smart investors pick promising AI businesses that have the potential to expand and offer abundant rewards, much as a knowledgeable farmer chooses the finest seeds to sow.

Chapter 4

Making Money with AI in the Future

Making money using AI has enormous promise in the future. As AI technology advances, new possibilities will emerge in industries such as automation, healthcare, finance, and others. From AI-powered services to investment possibilities, AI-driven enterprises and technologies will provide new ways to generate money. Those who accept and adapt to these developments will profit from the expanding AI economy. It's like being ready to reap the benefits of a never-ending field of opportunity.

AI Emerging Trends

Emerging AI trends serve as guideposts for the future of technology and its influence on different facets of our lives. These are the most recent and fascinating advances in the area of artificial intelligence. Here's a comprehensive look at some of these trends:

- XAI (Explainable AI):
  - What It Is: The goal of XAI is to make AI systems more visible and intelligible. Its primary goal is to develop AI models and algorithms that can explain their decision-making processes in human-readable language.
  - Why It Matters: XAI is vital for establishing confidence in AI systems, particularly in mission-critical applications such as healthcare and finance. It explains to people why AI makes certain suggestions or judgments.

- Artificial Intelligence in Healthcare:
  - What It Is: Artificial intelligence (AI) is transforming healthcare by providing early illness diagnosis, individualized treatment regimens, and predictive analytics. AI-powered medical imaging and diagnostic technologies are becoming more popular.
  - Why It Matters: AI in healthcare has the potential to save lives, save healthcare costs, and enhance patient care quality.

- Natural Language Processing (NLP) AI:
  - What It Is: NLP is concerned with training AI to comprehend and produce human language. More complex chatbots, language translation, and content development are all part of this trend.
  - Why It Matters: NLP is driving advancements in customer service, content production, and cross-language communication.

- AI in Self-Driving Cars:
  - What It Is: Artificial intelligence (AI) is a critical component of self-driving automobiles. Vehicles employ machine learning and computer vision to assess their surroundings and make real-time driving judgments.
  - Why It Matters: Self-driving cars have the potential to alter transportation by reducing accidents and increasing efficiency.

- Finance and AI:
  - What It Is: Artificial intelligence (AI) is used in financial services to identify fraud, perform algorithmic trading, evaluate risk, and provide tailored financial advice.

- Why It Matters: Artificial intelligence (AI) has the potential to enhance the accuracy and efficiency of financial operations, making them more accessible and secure for consumers and enterprises.

- Artificial Intelligence in Climate Change Solutions:
  - What It Is: Artificial intelligence (AI) is being used to combat climate change by optimizing energy consumption, forecasting environmental changes, and assisting with conservation efforts.
  - Why It Matters: AI has the potential to significantly reduce the effect of climate change while also encouraging sustainable habits.

- Artificial Intelligence in Education:
  - What It Is: AI is used to tailor learning experiences, give students adaptive feedback, and improve the educational process.
  - Why It Matters: AI in education has the potential to enhance student results and make learning more accessible to a broad range of students.

- Artificial Intelligence in Robotics:
  - What It Is: Artificial intelligence (AI) is powering powerful robots capable of difficult jobs ranging from manufacturing to healthcare and even home chores.
  - Why It Matters: AI-powered robots can boost productivity, do risky professions, and aid humans in a variety of ways.

- AI and Quantum Computing:
  - What It Is: The convergence of quantum computing with artificial intelligence holds the promise of solving difficult issues that were previously intractable for traditional computers.
  - Why It Matters: Quantum AI has the potential to revolutionize industries such as drug development, encryption, and materials research.

- Artificial Intelligence in Cybersecurity:
  - What It Is: Artificial intelligence (AI) is used to identify and react to cybersecurity threats in real-time, increasing the resilience of digital systems.
  - Why It Matters: Artificial intelligence improves the security of sensitive data and key infrastructure against cyberattacks.

These rising developments in artificial intelligence are altering the future of technology, promising to make our lives more efficient, safer, and more intelligent. They offer possibilities for innovation, investment, and good change in a variety of businesses and fields. Staying updated about these patterns is critical to harnessing the promise of AI in the next years, much like monitoring the horizon for hints of what's to come.

How Artificial Intelligence is Changing the Workplace

The way AI is affecting the workforce is similar to observing a shift in the way people work, which is being driven by advances in artificial intelligence. It is altering work responsibilities, duties, and the labor market. Here's a comprehensive overview of this seismic shift:

- Repetitive Task Automation: - What It Is: AI is automating regular and repetitive jobs like as data input, basic customer care, and assembly line labor.
  - Why It Matters: By freeing human workers from boring duties, they may

concentrate on more creative, complicated, and important work.

- 2. Increased Productivity: - What It Is: AI tools and software increase productivity by assisting workers in streamlining their job, making data-driven choices, and managing their time more effectively.

  - Why It Matters: AI enables workers to do jobs more quickly and precisely, resulting in enhanced overall productivity.

- What Is Personalized Learning and Development? AI-powered education and training systems provide customizable learning pathways that are tailored to workers' unique requirements and talents.

  - Why It's Important: This guarantees that employees get the information and skills needed to thrive in their professions, therefore contributing to their professional development.

- AI Assistants and Chatbots: - What They Are: AI-powered chatbots and virtual assistants are becoming more popular in customer service and administrative activities.

- Why It's Important: They give assistance, respond to requests, and handle regular communication, so increasing efficiency and response times.

- Advanced Data Analysis: What It Is: AI can analyze massive volumes of data to derive insights, assisting decision-making in a variety of sectors ranging from banking to healthcare.
    - Why It Matters: It allows employees to make better-educated, data-driven decisions and forecasts, improving overall decision quality.

- New employment positions: What They Are: AI is producing new employment positions such as AI trainers, data scientists, and automation experts to build, install, and maintain AI systems.
    - Why It Matters: These professions provide chances for skill development and professional progress in the area of artificial intelligence.

- Remote Work and Flexibility: - What It Is: AI makes flexible work arrangements more accessible by offering tools for communication, collaboration, and project management.

- Why It Matters: It enables workers to work from a variety of places and customize their work schedules to meet their specific demands.

- What It Is: AI may help address labor shortages in areas such as agriculture and manufacturing by aiding with jobs that need physical strength or accuracy

    - Why It Matters: It assists the industry in maintaining productivity while decreasing dependency on labor-intensive operations.

- Reskilling and Upskilling: What It Is: Organizations are investing in reskilling and upskilling programs to provide workers with the AI-related skills they will need in the future.

    - Why It's Important: This prepares the workforce for changes brought forth by AI and assures employability in a tech-driven employment market.

- Ethical and Human supervision: - What It Is: As AI systems become more common, there is a greater need for ethical concerns and human supervision in their deployment.

- Why It Matters: It guarantees that artificial intelligence is employed ethically and by social ideals.

The influence of artificial intelligence on the workforce is both transformational and collaborative. While technology automates certain processes, it also enables employees to thrive in their professions, promotes skill development, and opens up new possibilities in AI-related domains. Adaptation and continual learning, like navigating and exploring new and dynamic terrain, are critical to prospering in this changing work environment.

Ethical implications for profiting from AI

Ethical issues for generating money with AI serve as a moral compass for how AI technologies are created, deployed, and commercialized. These factors are critical to ensuring that AI-powered enterprises and practices serve society and uphold human values. Here's a comprehensive guide to these ethical considerations:

- Transparency: - What It Is: Being transparent about how AI systems make judgments and analyze data is what transparency in AI is all about. It is all about giving people precise information.
  - Why It Matters: Transparency fosters confidence, enabling consumers to comprehend AI thinking, and aids in making educated decisions.

- Privacy: - What Is It? Individual privacy is protected by safeguarding personal data, gaining permission for data use, and ensuring that AI systems do not violate privacy rights.
  - Why It's Important: Privacy is a basic right, and ethical AI enterprises place a premium on data security and user permission.

- Fairness: What It Is: In AI, fairness involves ensuring that AI systems do not discriminate against humans based on their race, gender, age, or other protected characteristics.

- Why It's Important: Fair AI fosters equality of opportunity while avoiding the reinforcement of existing biases and prejudice.

- Accountability: - What It Is: Accountability for AI systems is accepting responsibility for their activities, including addressing and correcting any damage they may do.
  - Why It Matters: Accountability holds AI inventors and users accountable for the outcomes of AI technology.

- Security: What It Is: AI security entails safeguarding AI systems from hacking, breaches, and abuse to protect users and society.
  - Why It Matters: Security is critical for maintaining confidence and preventing AI from being used maliciously.

- Bias Reduction: - What It Is: To achieve equal results, bias reduction in AI entails actively finding and removing biases in training data and algorithms.
  - Why It's Important: It is critical to address biases to prevent unjust treatment and choices made by AI systems.

- Permission and Control: - What It Is: Users should have control over their interactions with AI systems, and their permission for data use should be acquired.

   - Why It's Important: Giving people power and receiving permission respects their autonomy and choice.

- Long-Term Consequences: - What It Is: Ethical issues go beyond short-term financial rewards. AI companies should also think about the long-term social, economic, and environmental consequences of their goods and services.

   - Why It's Important: Thinking on the larger implications secures AI's beneficial role in society.

- Education and Awareness: - What It Is: Raising awareness and knowledge of AI's potential and limits, both among workers and the general public, is critical.

   - Why It Matters: Knowledgeable stakeholders are better suited to employ AI responsibly and ethically.

- Regulatory Compliance: What Is It? Adherence to AI-related rules and regulations, as well as data protection and ethics, is critical for AI enterprises.
  - Why It's Important: Compliance guarantees that operations are lawful and ethical, avoiding any legal concerns and fines.

AI ethics guarantee that profiting from AI does not come at the price of social well-being or individual rights. Ethical AI companies aspire to build goods and services that match with human values, encourage trust, and contribute positively to technological innovation. Ethical AI firms, like responsible businesses, promote values that help both their financial line and society as a whole.

Conclusion

"How to Make Money with AI" is more than simply a financial success book; it's a road map for thriving in the ever-changing environment of artificial intelligence. This book provides you with the information and insights you need to harness the potential of AI for financial advantage, from understanding the principles of AI to spotting possibilities, from building AI-powered products to investing in AI-driven firms.

It's not only about generating money as AI continues to impact businesses; it's about adapting, inventing, and aligning with ethical issues. The future of creating money with AI is a fascinating adventure, and this book equips you with the skills and expertise to navigate it.

In this age of technological upheaval, your ability to use AI ethically and successfully may lead to financial success while also benefiting society. You'll be able to maximize AI's promise while still being a responsible and forward-thinking member of the AI-driven economy if you've read these pages.

So, go on this path, and may your quest for financial success using artificial intelligence be both enjoyable and cognizant of the world-changing potential that lie ahead.